STEAM MEMORIES : 1950's – 196

BR STANDARDS AT LAR

Copyright Book Law Publications 2010
ISBN 978-1-907094-93-4

INTRODUCTION

This album contains the photographic work of four different railway enthusiasts who each strove to get the best from their cameras in an age when film was both expensive and hard to obtain. The resulting mixture is both pleasing and rewarding for there are a number of locations rarely photographed whilst others simply tell their story in striking tones of black and white.

We have managed to put together an album showing the BR Standard classes at their best and worse; the expectant hopes (and fears) of the new, coupled with the disillusionment and downright waste of the 1960s.

The photographers in question are the late David Dalton whose pictures form the bulk of the illustrations. Next is Ron Hodge who brings some nice surprises to bear. Two other gentlemen who are no longer with us but whose work needs no introduction are Don Beecroft and Keith Pirt. Thank you gentlemen for getting out and about during those heady years of change.

(Cover picture) **Cl.4 No.76088 at Millhouses shed.** *Keith Pirt.*

(previous page) **During the last few years of the Nottingham (Victoria) to Marylebone passenger services a number of 'Britannias' showed their faces on the working in place of the failing 'Royal Scots' which, even at the leisurely pace of the old GC main line, found it hard to hold themselves together. So, as the 'Scots' went the 'Brits' came. First there were those from Willesden such as No.70004 WILLIAM SHAKESPEARE heading an Up train at Leicester (Central) on 17th July 1964. Later came the Banbury 'Brits' with the big BR1C tenders which were better to handle the arduous engine diagrams as the water troughs were taken out. Eventually of course the whole railway was taken out so this picture from 1964 is real history.** *David Dalton.*

Printed and bound by The Amadeus Press, Cleckheaton, West Yorkshire
First published in the United Kingdom by Book Law Publications, 382 Carlton Hill, Nottingham, NG4 1JA

Since September 1963 Exmouth Junction engine shed had been part of the Western Region. Under the new regime the depot had lost its previous Southern Region coding 72A in favour of 83D (the old Plymouth Laira code) and came under Newton Abbot supervision. Except for the introduction of a few Pannier tanks on branch services, the former SR allocation at the Exeter depot did not alter that much. Evidence of that status quo came be seen in this 29th March 1964 view of Cl.4 2-6-4T No.80064 sandwiched between two ex Southern 2-6-0 tender engines. No.80064 had transferred to 83D in June 1962 from Tonbridge - Exmouth Junction had in fact been its fourth SR shed since arriving from the London Midland Region two and a half years previously - and resided at the depot until its closure to steam in June 1965. During its time at Exmouth Junction, the Cl.4 did most of its work in North Cornwall and was equally at home on passenger and freight duties. The years of 1964 and 1965 were perilous ones for the Exmouth Junction Standard classes; there numbers were such that there was not enough work to go round therefore the slightest breakdown usually rendered the locomotive redundant and it was condemned. A number of the 83D Cl.4 tanks ended their days after trivial mechanical defects saw them failed; No.80064 was lucky in that it escaped to Bristol Barrow Road shed in June 1965 only to be condemned in August. That large dent running along the lower section of its tank did not have any detrimental effect to its existence whilst at Exeter. Luck appears to have followed this engine around throughout its life because when it was sold for scrap, in late September 1965, it was purchased by a certain breakers yard located in South Wales.....
David Dalton.

Besides the obvious extra boiler (pre-heater) beneath the conventional main boiler, and the associated side chimney fitted to the Crosti 9Fs, they also had both clack valves on the right side of the main boiler which they all kept after rebuilding to the orthodox design. No.92026 shows off its clacks in this 7th November 1959 view at Cricklewood, some two months after being rebuilt at Crewe - the first engine to undergo the rebuilding. A spare boiler - No.1903 - was built for ten Crosti engines in October 1961 but was apparently only used by No.92024. The ten Crosti type boilers (BR12 Nos.1148 to 1157), even after rebuilding were used only on locomotives Nos.92020 to 92029. When they were running in their original guise, the ten Crosti engines weighed approximately four tons more than their 'normal' classmates but after conversion their weight was reduced by nearly five tons. *David Dalton.*

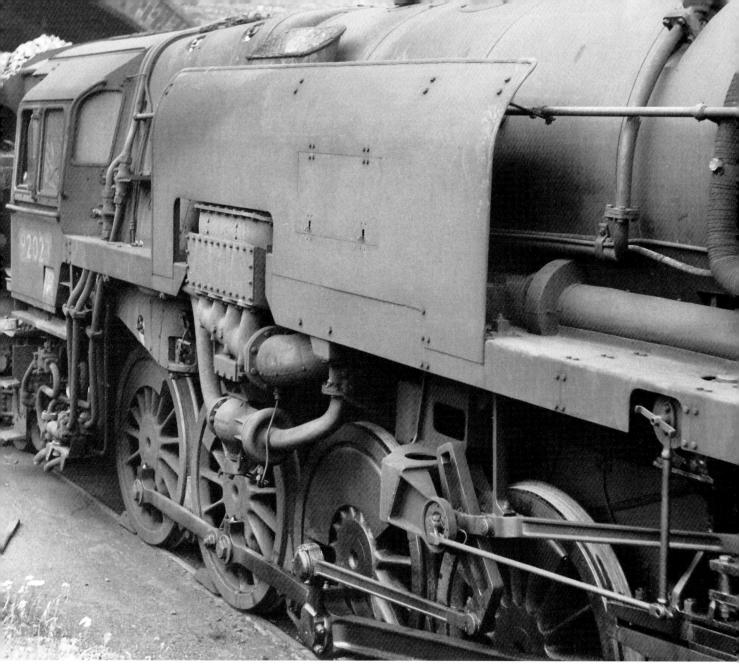

Close-up of the large smoke deflector eventually fitted to all ten of the Crosti equipped 9F 2-10-0s. This is No.92023 at Wellingborough shed on 3rd August 1956, nearly six months after the modification took place. Note the hatch, which opened inwards, cut into the middle of the deflector to enable shed staff to reach and fill the sand hopper. Notice also the two wedges placed under the fourth and fifth coupled wheels!! *Ron Hodge.*

After receiving its last heavy overhaul - Heavy Intermediate - No.92110 gets ready for a week of testing at Crewe works on 21st May 1966 prior being released to traffic on the 26th May. Having started life working from Toton shed in October 1956 and spending the next eight years working from various depots situated along the length of the former Midland main line between London and the Erewash valley, the 2-10-0 now wears the shed plate of its final home 12A Kingmoor. Its move from the East Midlands in September 1964 sent No.92110 initially to Newton Heath but it left there after just eight months for Carlisle. This particular HI overhaul will ensure eighteen months of work for the 9F before its premature withdrawal in December 1967. Incredibly, when the end of steam working took effect on BR, none of the 9Fs were amongst those last working engines which comprised Stanier products in the main. In the background a bunch of enthusiasts stroll towards the Paint shop where the doors are invitingly open, something of a rarity during the last ten years or so of steam locomotive repairs at Crewe. *David Dalton.*

Just about to enter the environs of Leicester's Central station, Annesley 9F No.92032 heads for home with a train of empty mineral wagons on Friday 18th September 1964. The sun is beginning to set on what was promising to be one of those warm late summer evenings when, for many, peace descends after the day's toil is ended and relaxation can begin to take effect. However, the sun was also setting on this particular regular 9F working - the Annesley to Woodford coal trains and their return working known along the former GCR main line as 'windcutters'. The service comprised numerous trains run to an accelerated timetable each weekday between the East Midlands coal districts and the southern distribution point for London and points west at Woodford. For many years the service was worked by Thompson O1 2-8-0s under the auspices of the Eastern Region. These were supplemented by the BR Standard 9Fs received at Annesley from February 1957 onwards. Eventually, when the London Midland Region took over the former Great Central main line and the ER routes around the Nottingham area, the O1s were replaced by Stanier 8F 2-8-0s but the 9Fs stayed on for a while. However, with the LMR authorities doing all in their power to divert traffic or cease the GC main line services completely, freight and passenger, the fast running coal trains were given up and the 9Fs dispersed to Midland line sheds, storage or to depots in the north-west of England. Our subject here was designated to transfer to Kirkby-in-Ashfield in June 1965 but went into store for a couple of weeks prior to being reallocated to Birkenhead. Its external condition in this photograph is somewhat grimy and it probably remained that way for the rest of its life which ended in April 1967. *David Dalton.*

This is not a rail tour just an ordinary express train working over the Lakeland Fells in August 1964 with 'Britannia' No.70035 RUDYARD
8 **KIPLING - yes the plates are still in situ - in charge and putting in a nice turn of speed to compliment the exhaust.** *David Dalton.*

In the days when naming a locomotive actually meant something to both those involved in the ceremony and those interested parties looking on, the identity of certain locomotives was actually kept secret - well sort of - from the public. However, once a name was unveiled a great deal of publicity would be gained and generated. But, that was in the days when we, as a nation, had different values, when we were easily pleased and, we were happy with our lot! Such was the setting and the Britain when the first of the 'Clan' class Pacifics No.72000 was ready for naming but had its new identity hidden until the actual event took place. This is Crewe works Paint shop, or at least the south wall of the place where most of the LMS official locomotive portraits were taken. The chimneys in the background, appearing to project from the Clans' tender, are the boiler house chimneys keeping the Paint shop warm. Oh yes, the date - 12th December 1951. *David Dalton.* 9

Accelerating away from Perth with a Glasgow bound express on the evening of 29th July 1966, Cl.5 No.73145 passes a line of withdrawn ex LMS Class 5s stored across the main line from the motive power depot. Soon the BR Standard would join its elder sisters because its withdrawal was only weeks away. After nine years working from St Rollox depot and covering the same duties as seen here, No.73145 transferred to Eastfield depot in January 1966 along with another St Rollox 'Std.5' No.73146. Of the ten Caprotti Standard Cl.5s housed at St Rollox since their introduction in 1957, three had been withdrawn in 1965, one (73154) went to Stirling in December 1965 whilst the other four remained at 65B and of those No.73151 was withdrawn in August 1966 whilst the other three moved on to Stirling with the closure of St Rollox looming in December 1966. However, all had been condemned by the end of the year except No.73146 which survived until May 1967 at Motherwell. *David Dalton.*

Was this picture posed? It is certainly a nice composition along with a fabulous location in which to find a BR Standard locomotive. This is Canbusavie Platform, a little used but nevertheless necessary halt on the Dornoch branch on Tuesday 5th August 1958. The train is the normal make-up for the branch consisting two vans, a brake and a passenger brake and is en route from The Mound to Dornoch terminus. The usual motive power working this former Highland Railway branch at this period was former Western Region 0-6-0PT No.1646 which had arrived during April 1957 to take over from the condemned ex HR 0-4-4T No.55053 which had 'given up the ghost' a few months previously. It was during this stop-gap between the demise of the HR tank and the arrival of the unusual replacement from Wales that No.78052 was brought in to help. In February 1957 it was allocated to Helmsdale shed (60C) and worked the service alone until the Pannier took over. However, the Cl.2 was kept on as spare engine - there was always two just in case - until another Pannier, No.1649, arrived from Bristol in August 1958. No.78052's eighteen month stint in the Highland idyll was over and it returned south after holding the mantle of being the most northerly allocated BR Standard on record. *David Dalton.*

Four days later and No.78052 and WR Pannier No.1646 meet at the southern end (it was actually the north-western end but the direction of running is in a southerly, Up direction towards Inverness) of The Mound station platform for changeover. From the looks of things the crews are also changing footplates. The 0-6-0PT would continue south through the junction in the distance and stop well beyond to enable the tender engine to proceed over the junction so that it can then reverse onto the branch and take up its duties as branch engine whilst the Pannier sets off to the north and Helmsdale shed for a washout and any other maintenance. This would have been one of the last stints on the branch for the Standard because it would soon be en route from Helmsdale to Inverness and eventually Edinburgh. However, the 2-6-0 would not be leaving the Highlands for good and would return for a four year residence but this time south of the Moray Firth at Aviemore shed. Note that No.78052 has already turned at Helmsdale shed to enable a more comfortable journey south for its crew when the day arrives for transfer. *David Dalton.*

After coaling and fire cleaning, note those hot ashes and clinker on the ground, No.70000 reverses to the water column at Parkeston shed on 5th May 1957. BRITANNIA has just worked in from Liverpool Street with the 8.00 a.m. *THE DAY CONTINENTAL* and afterwards returned to London with the 1.15 p.m. *SCANDINAVIAN*. The back lighting of the picture along with the appliance, discarded fire irons and the adjacent unidentified locomotive give this illustration a nice 'feel.' Note the small inscription on the left of the bufferbeam which states 'R 7.' This writer is uncertain as to the meaning of the figures or indeed if what is visible was the whole thing. Any answers, or even ideas, to the Publisher please via the usual channels. *Ron Hodge.*

Providing motive power for the Leicester West Bridge branch was once the responsibility of Coalville shed and towards the end of steam working in the Midlands the shed acquired a few Standard Cl.2 tender engines as replacements for the ancient and withdrawn former Midland Railway 0-6-0 tender engines which used to work the line. One of the BR 2-6-0s was No.78028 seen here at Glenfield on 11th April 1966 and seemingly struggling to keep going but it was good for another ten months yet! By the date of the photograph the engine had actually reallocated to Leicester Midland shed but within three months it had been transferred to Toton where it went into store prior to moving off to Bolton in November. It was condemned in February 1967. *David Dalton.*

Although not the sharpest of photographs, it is worth including in this album for its curiosity value. Brand new No.78007 was en route from Darlington on delivery to Swindon to work on the Western Region. Annesley shed, situated along its route via the former GC main line, was chosen as a stopping off and checking point where the engine could spend the night prior to carrying on southwards to the WR. The Cl.2 must have visited at a most opportune time for the depot because they required motive power to run the Dido (there was always a shortage of suitable engines for the service it seems) so low and behold here it is on 27th March 1953 at the former Great Northern station's Up platform doing the honours whilst Swindon is probably wondering what has happened to their new charge. Annesley didn't care; Swindon was on another planet and besides a day on the Dido would sort out any gremlins that the low mileage 2-6-0 might have! No.78007 eventually arrived at Swindon works who then sent it to Oswestry none the wiser. *David Dalton.*

Hopefully, if this picture is cropped with care, the left side of the illustration will remain to reveal to the reader the pair of BR1F tenders awaiting their engines at Swindon works on 24th February 1957. Without that half-inch wide strip of photograph this particular picture could make headline news in one of the monthly mags' with the headline running something like 'Brand new 9F undergoes trials with Churchward/Collett? tender at Swindon' followed by 'seen in this extraordinary view as captured by a secret camera on Sunday 24th February 1957, the 2-10-0 was coming off the traverser and making its way towards the works exit with the thirty year old tender in tow.' Anyway, No.92095 was, as can be seen, positioned next to a former GW tender waiting to be coupled to one of the new BR1F tenders on the left. After which the engine/tender combination collectively known from this point onwards as No.92095, were destined for the Eastern Region and Annesley shed in particular. After eight years at Annesley it transferred to Kirkby-in-Ashfield in June 1965 but never worked there going instead into store. In May 1966 steam was raised once again and the 9F moved to Warrington but at less than six months at Dallam it was condemned and later hauled away for scrap. *David Dalton.*

Cl.5 No.73025 got to Cardiff Canton from Blackpool via Shrewsbury. It had spent nearly two years at the seaside from new before moving to Salop in September 1953 for a ten month stint. Thereafter it worked for the Western Region from various sheds until April 1966 when it went to Agecroft prior to transferring to the shed which seemed to be the spiritual home of the BR Standard Cl.5 – Patricroft. *Ron Hodge.*

Cl.2 No.78040 was one of five (78040 to 78044) which went new to Bank Hall shed in Liverpool during December 1954. Three of them stayed put at 27A until the early 60s but two, 78040 here and 78043 'jumped ship' the latter in November 1956 to nearby Aintree whereas our subject got a bit more adventurous three months later and travelled east to Wigan where it was photographed stabled outside its new home at the former Lancashire & Yorkshire depot known as Wigan Central. Long time resident No.78063 looks on from inside the shed whilst another unidentified member of the class stands alongside. Considering the shed here was a run-down ramshackle affair, its allocation was fairly modern at this time with LMS and BR Standard classes in the majority. *David Dalton.*

The other side of No.78040 when it was part of the Bank Hall stud. *Ron Hodge.*

At least Crewe knew how to present a new 9F for the weekend visitor. Here outside the Paint shop coupled to a BR1C tender, No.92155 offers a gleaming mirror finish painted livery to the camera in early November 1957. Even the wheels appear burnished so perhaps the engine is ready for exhibition somewhere although the winter months are not usually chosen for outside exhibiting. Behind the tender is a Western Region WD 2-8-0 which, like all the Austerity 2-8-0s overhauled at Crewe, would not normally be allowed into the Paint shop and would undergo painting in the yard outside or within the Erecting shop, depending on the weather. Exhibition or not, the 9F ended up at Saltley before the month was out then in August 1966 it was transferred to Speke Junction but did very little there until withdrawn three months later just nine years old! *David Dalton.*

Ex works Doncaster style: Cl.4 No.76109 poses in the works yard during August 1957 prior to running-in and delivery to the Scottish Region. The tender is partially coaled and scrap wood in the cab signifies the lighting of its first fire. Note the lack of any power classification markings on the cab side, also the wrong facing BR crest! *Neville Stead coll..*

The Plant Centenary Exhibition at Doncaster Works was held during late September 1953 and a number of locomotives, old and new, were on display for the public. Besides the obvious Gresley products, A4, V2, etc., at least two BR Standard locomotives took part in the exhibition, a Cl.4 2-6-0 760XX (possibly No.76025 which was new at the time but just out of frame on the right) a class of engine then being built at Doncaster, and No.70000 BRITANNIA which although not a product of the 'Plant' was at that time a showpiece of British Railways motive power standardisation. In this view outside the Paint shop, BRITANNIA appears to be taking centre stage but the quality of its appearance looks somewhat indifferent for such a 'prestige' exhibit but it was a Stratford engine at the time. Also in the picture EM1 Bo-Bo electric No.26020 (ex Gorton Paint shop) can be seen on the left. A4 No.60022 MALLARD is just visible behind No.70000. *David Dalton.*

En route from Doncaster to its new home on the Southern Region, Cl.4 No.76053 has called in at March on 24th April 1955, or so it appears. In truth, the 2-6-0 might just be involved in a Doncaster running-in turn which has brought it down to the Cambridgeshire yard prior to working back to Doncaster with another train ready to be 'signed off' and sent on its way to Redhill. Note the Route Availability legend (RA 4) beneath the number on the cabside; not much use on the SR but old habits, etc. The SR based members of this class were coupled to both types of tender afforded the Class 4 2-6-0s, the high capacity (water) BR1B as coupled to No.76053 here, and the lower capacity BR2 type. There was a significant different in the working order weight of some nine tons between the two. Managing twelve years service on the Southern, No.76053 never came this far north again and was scrapped at Cashmore's yard in Newport, Monmouthshire. *David Dalton.*

Reversing out of Paddington terminus after bringing in a morning express from Cardiff, Canton based 'Brit' No.70027 RISING STAR gets some admiring glances from the throng of 'spotters' at the platform end on 15th June 1957. By now the engine has had its smoke deflectors altered to incorporate the hand holds in place of the rails, and the new BR emblem has been applied to the tender. From here the Pacific would go to the locomotive servicing yard at Ranelagh Bridge (less than half a mile away) to be turned, coaled and watered for its return working which was probably the 1.55 p.m. express to Swansea and Pembroke Dock. Note the amount and height of the coal still in the tender bunker. *David Dalton.*

In the days before the handrails on the smoke deflectors of the Western Region 'Britannias' were altered to hand holds, No.70029 SHOOTING STAR heads Down train No.173 *THE RED DRAGON* at Paddington on 24th September 1955. Deprived of any 'Kings', Canton shed used their allocation of 'Brits' for all of their prestige trains and made the best of them. Perhaps only Norwich depot could be said to have given the BR Pacifics more credence. *Ron Hodge.*

This is the kind of work to which the Cl.2 tender engines were imminently suited - station pilot duties. No.78030 is at a dull and damp Crewe station on 19th May 1957. Starting life on similar work at Preston in September 1954, No.78030 transferred to Crewe North in April 1956 - one of the few small engines attached to the depot which was full of big engines - and moved to Crewe South shed in October 1964 to carry on the station pilot work from there. Withdrawal took place in October 1965, aged eleven years. *David Dalton.*

Halfway through its miserably short life, we have this rather striking view of very dirty Cl.4 No.76084 which is ready to depart with a passenger service from a station somewhere in East Lancashire on 24th February 1962. Lower Darwen was this engine's first shed but at the time of this photograph the 2-6-0 was having a second, longer - six years against sixteen months first time around - residence at the East Lancashire depot. Another preserved example, No.76084 had the luck to be sent to Barry scrap yard from its last shed at Springs Branch. *David Dalton.*

All the staff at Wellingborough depot must have thought 'What have we done to deserve this lot' when given the keys to ten new 9F 2-10-0s during the summer of 1955. By that fateful year, the shed had already received a dozen or so 9Fs and everyone at 15A from fitters to footplatemen had welcomed the big engines with open arms - 'the Garratts were going so bring on more 9Fs' might have been the overwhelming cry. However, Wellingborough was in for a shock of sorts - the Crosti sort. This is the eighth member of the ten strong 'Crosti boiler gang' as turned-out by Crewe works upon an unsuspecting Operating Department in 1955. It was a class which turned out to be somewhat egregious to all concerned with their running and maintenance. No.92027, pictured outside the Paint shop on 26th June 1955, looked quite tasty for all intents and purposes but history was to prove otherwise. *David Dalton.*

By the time No.92220 EVENING STAR was presented to the world in 1960, the Crosti boiler fiasco was all but resolved but then another crisis loomed for British Railway - what to do with all these new 2-10-0s we have lying around idling? That might be deemed the case here on 26th March 1961 at, apparently, Cardiff (Canton) but more likely to be at Gloucester (Barnwood)?. In the latter case the 9F would of course be visiting and one of that depot's 4F 0-6-0s decorates the right side of the illustration whilst a WR 4-6-0 stands at the rear of the 'last one'. Canton shed used No.92220 sparingly and by the summer of 1962 managed to get rid of it to Bath (Green Park) from where it could work over the Somerset & Dorset away from harms way because by this time every shed seemed to be treating it with kid gloves and reverence. It worked the S&D for two months before transferring to Old Oak Common who after a few weeks sent it to Oxford who kept it for the winter of 62-63 before packing it off to Green Park for another stint on the S&D. At least this time No.92220 managed to get to the end of the Summer WTT before moving on in October 1963, back to Cardiff but to East Dock. In March 1965 it was officially 'stored' according to the Western Region but the truth was that it had done very little work since returning to Cardiff. During that same month it was withdrawn whilst in store. Where it went and for how long is something of a mystery after that date. This writer remembers seeing it from a passing train languishing in a siding opposite Pontypool Road shed in 1966, windows broken, nameplates removed and looking thoroughly dejected - no way to treat such an icon. Luckily the authorities eventually got their act together and the rest is - terrific!
David Dalton.

Cl.4 No.75079 is stabled at its home shed Basingstoke on Sunday 17th August 1958 but visitors and interlopers of all kind disturb the otherwise tranquil nature of the three road shed. Like most engines on the SR at that time, No.75079 wears a thick coating of grime, only the new diesel shunter and something ex works at the side of the shed stand out; everything else is a mingled blur of dirt. The Cl.4 spent nearly seven years at this depot from June 1956 until a transfer - shed closure - in March 1963 took it to Eastleigh for the rest of its days. *David Dalton.*

Cl.4 No.75024 was a Western engine through and through. It was built at Swindon, it was allocated to the WR from new and for the next eleven years and six months worked from WR depots. In February 1959, just prior to transferring from Oxford to Swindon, it had green livery applied, complete with lining! In this pre-green livery photograph taken circa 1955, the 4-6-0 is stabled at Oswestry its home shed from December 1953 to February 1958 when it went to Shrewsbury. Most of its time at Oswestry was spent working over the former Cambrian lines to the west coast of Wales and later during its career it ended up at Machynlleth twice but both times for just short periods. In December 1966 it broke nearly all of its ties with the WR and moved to Stoke-on-Trent, then later to Tebay. The one reminder of its Swindon 'heritage' was the green livery which it kept and even had a refreshing coat applied in July 1965 during an overhaul at Cowlairs! *Ron Hodge.*

Minus nameplates but otherwise intact, 'Brit' No.70025, formerly WESTERN STAR, makes a dramatic exit from Crewe with a northbound express in 1966. Even the chime whistle has been brought into play as the confident crew peer out from the cab. Hopefully the Pacific did not let them down. *David Dalton.*

Feast your eyes on this because seven years and six months after the photograph was taken on 7th April 1957, this Cl.2 tank was condemned and cut up at Crewe. We are in the works yard at Darlington and the 2-6-2T is just three days away from being released into traffic. The destination of No.84024, once it had left the care of Darlington works and the running-in tasks, was Ashford shed from where the motor-fitted Cl.2 would take up employment, along with Nos.84020, 84021, 84022 and 84023, on various jobs previously performed by Class H tanks for which they were replacements. Although fitted to work push-pull services, these BR tank engines were basically useless for such duties in East Kent because they worked on the vacuum system whereas the Southern stock was controlled by a compressed air system (Did anyone care about those things within BR? It seems not!). The other Darlington built Cl.2 tanks, Nos.84025 to 84029, would follow them to Kent carrying out similar duties but from Ramsgate shed. 1961 proved to be their last year working on the SR most of the Darlington built engines had been passed from pillar to post during the few years south of the Thames and in September they were all transferred to the London Midland Region during the topsy-turvy period when many Standards were being sent from other regions to work on the SR. In a somewhat unusual move, even by BR standards at the time, Nos.84021 to 84024 were all transferred to Crewe during July 1962 to be used as works shunters. Their end, when it came, was swift and uncompromising. On 5th September 1964 all four were condemned and after broken up at their last place of employment. Note the newly applied but wrong facing BR emblem adorning the tank side. *David Dalton.* 33

Heading a Liverpool (Lime Street) to Manchester (Oxford Road) via Warrington (Bank Quay, Low Level) stopping service, on Saturday 14th April 1962, Cl.2 tank No.84001 pauses by the water column at the latter station, just in case. Allocated by now to Warrington's Dallam shed, along with sister No.84000, No.84001 became a regular performer on this stopping service which had a somewhat leisurely terminus to terminus timing. The first twenty of the class, all motor-fitted, were built at Crewe to be used by the LMR at various locations throughout the region. After service at Bolton, Wrexham, Chester and Birkenhead, this 2-6-2T arrived at Warrington in the summer of 1961 in time to work the final year of this particular steam hauled passenger service. There was a certain tragedy about this class - they came along too late but had every refinement required to be fully employed in world thirty years in the past; the enginemen liked them, but their full potential was never achieved. No.84001 was put into storage at Dallam from early September 1962 until its transfer to Llandudno Junction later in the year. *David Dalton.*

No.84001 has reached its destination, one of the two terminal platforms at the rebuilt and by now fully functioning Manchester (Oxford Road) station - 14th April 1962. The service on which No.84001 is employed would soon cease and another job would have to occupy the Cl.2 until the end of summer and the imminent storage. It was something of a rarity to capture BR Standard tanks on film at this particular location in 1962. *David Dalton.*

"What do you want?" might be the words coming out of the surprised looking Boilersmiths mouth inside the Erecting shop at Brighton works on Wednesday 28th September 1955, as he toils with some component located inside the smokebox of soon-to-be Cl.4 2-6-4T No.80125. Brighton built the bulk of the Cl.4 tank engines, some 130 in all compared with fifteen at Derby and ten at Doncaster. No.80125 went new to Stirling where it put in some good work on the main line to Perth and south to Glasgow also on the branch to Crieff. Requiring minor works attention in July 1964, No.80125 was withdrawn by the Scottish Region but the engine was promptly re-instated (September) by the LM Region who wanted the locomotive at Lostock Hall. The 'second life' was short because during the following October, whilst visiting Crewe for overhaul, it was condemned for good and sold to a scrap merchant in Liverpool. *Ron Hodge.*

Here is the last of the BR Standard Cl.2 2-6-2 tank engines, No.84029, in the course of being erected at Darlington works on 7th April 1957. The engine was complete and ready for traffic on 11th June 1957. The notice hanging from the bufferbeam reads...J.Holdsworth 262T 2BR No.10. *David Dalton.*

This is Cl.4 No.80005 - you'll have to take my word for it - hauling a seven coach Aberdeen to Banff service at Golf Club House Halt on a glorious Saturday, 8th June 1957. This was day-trip country for Aberdonians and a number seem to be strolling towards the beach in this fine postcard type photograph. The view is north-westward, looking over Boyndie Bay towards Knock Head with the settlement of Whitehill to its the south. The beach and its bay look very inviting in June but shortly thereafter any similarity with a similar named location 'Down Under' ends. Our train is running over the metals of the former Great North of Scotland Railway but this stretch of line to Banff (which is to the right of the frame, and could boast a one-road engine shed until July 1964) had origins back to 1859 when the erstwhile Banff, Portsoy & Strathisla Railway built the picturesque route. The 'halt' with the long name opened in October 1913 as a request stop only and then only seasonal ; it closed 6th July 1964. Alas, this railway is no more but the bay and its promontory are still giving visual joy to visitors, perhaps even Australians eager to view the original Boyndie! So, where does the BR Standard Cl.4 feature in all this? Our 2-6-4T was of course one of the Derby batch which were put into traffic rather late and only appeared during the latter quarter of 1952, long after Brighton had turned out its first thirty-odd examples from July 1951 onwards. It first depot was Kittybrewster where work such as this was available until it transferred away to Glasgow in July 1959. Thereafter it was all downhill for the Cl.4 although it did a bit of uphill work when attached to Beattock shed between March and November 1965. *David Dalton.*

New England's No.92040 runs through Little Bytham with the Cliffe-Uddington bulk cement train 18th August 1962. Although a regular New England working for the few years it ran whilst that depot existed, Type 3 diesel-electric Bo-Bo locomotives from the Southern Region depot at Hither Green eventually took over the daily working for its entire distance from Kent to Glasgow. *David Dalton.*

During the last four or so years of steam working on British Railways, a number of railtours were run by various railway enthusiast societies. Besides having 'celebrity' locomotives as the motive power, as in many cases, members of the Britannia class were responsible for hauling quite a few such tours during the period in question. This is Crewe South's No.70012 JOHN OF GAUNT (the nameplates were in fact wooden, though nicely crafted ones, and were fitted in place of the metal originals which had been removed some time previously) at Cleethorpes on 2nd October 1965 'running round' after arrival in the resort with the RCTS *NORTH LINCOLNSHIRE RAIL TOUR*. Consisting six coaches, the tour had started from Nottingham (Midland) in late morning then spent the afternoon traversing various routes in Lincolnshire from Boston up to Cleethorpes (reversal), then on past Grimsby and into New Holland where another reversal was necessary. Afterwards it was off to Barnetby, Wrawby Junction, Market Rasen, Lincoln and the LD&ECR to Warsop Junction, Mansfield (Town), Pye Bridge, Trowell, Toton, Beeston and Nottingham (Midland). Four different footplate crews from Colwick, Immingham, Langwith Junction and Nottingham were involved. The 'Brit' performed excellently but had little chance to stretch those long legs.

(opposite) No.70012 gets into reversal mode at New Holland. Note the express headlamps! *David Dalton.*

To say that the sixty-five Cl.2 2-6-0 tender engines were under-utilised by British Railways would be a definite understatement. This is No.78026 at Canklow shed 30th July 1955, the tender of classmate No.78027 is visible on the right. With some of the Standards there was a constant scratching of the head within the Operating Department as they sought out appropriate jobs for the 'limousines' as some of them became known - a reputation gained no doubt by virtue of their comfortable and draught free cabs. That the majority of the class lasted into 1966 and many into the following year is testimony to their being the 'enginemens best friends'. They were ideal for station pilot work and carriage pilot duties where a lot of 'hanging around' was performed between jobs. There were great for trip working and shunting. They did little in the way of passenger train haulage by 1962 as the diesel multiple unit fleet had grown enough to take over the remaining services. So, what became of the Canklow pair? No.78026 transferred to Scotland in January 1962 and never came back. No.78027 went to the Eastern Region in August 1962 but ended its day on the LMR. *Ron Hodge.*

Sharing the same road as an unidentified 'Duchess', 'Britannia' No.70046 ANZAC rests at Crewe North shed before taking on a Holyhead bound express at some date in 1963. According to the shedplate the Pacific was allocated to Holyhead, something which had taken place three times during the engines lifetime. It had also been shedded at seven other LMR depots but none more so than Holyhead. No.70046 was late in receiving its name and ran nameless for more than five years before a little ceremony in September 1959 saw the small ANZAC nameplates fitted to its large smoke deflectors. Less than seven years later the plates were removed at its final depot, **Kingmoor**. *David Dalton.*

'Britannia' No.70011 HOTSPUR has just reversed onto the stock of *THE EAST ANGLIAN* at Norwich (Thorpe) on Friday 20th September 1957. The Pacific looks rather clean and this was probably down to a shed clean rather than an ex-works sheen. The arrival of the Britannias on the former Great Eastern main lines out of Liverpool Street really speeded up express services such as this. They ruled these services for nearly a decade before the coming of the English Electric Type 4 diesel-electrics sent them onto secondary work.

(opposite) The front end of HOTSPUR on that same day with the train headboard proudly displayed on the top of the smokebox door for all to see. Both *David Dalton.*

Here is another Norwich (Thorpe) view, this from 28th September 1957 with Stratford 'Brit' No.70002 GEOFFREY CHAUCER heading a Liverpool Street express made up of Gresley and Thompson vehicles.

The date is sometime in March 1967. The location is York motive power depot. The subject - two woebegone 9Fs, Nos.92060 and 92097, en route from Tyne Dock shed to Draper's scrap yard in Hull. To enable virtual trouble-free running between their departure and arrival venues both engines have their motion stripped down and placed in their respective tenders, however, the huge connecting rods which were too long to be accommodated in the coal bunker, have been secured to the running plate. Note the air pumps still gracing the sides of the engines. York shed was a favoured stopping off point for engines being taken to Draper's from depots in the north-east whilst the yard was operational. both images *David Dalton.*

With just some glass from the cab windows and the shed plate missing, everything else is intact on the one-off BR Standard 8P Pacific No.71000 **DUKE OF GLOUCESTER** as it resides outside the Paint shop at Crewe works on 21st May 1966. Thirty-odd years on from the day this scene was captured and the big engine literally rose from the ashes. Second time around it was better than the first time. May it live forever. *David Dalton.*

Seemingly grounded by the ash and clinker surrounding it, Cl.4 No.80143 was still active at Nine Elms when this photograph was taken in March 1967. Like all the engines allocated to the London depot at this time, the 2-6-4T was in a deplorable external condition which would normally by a sign of storage after withdrawal but No.80143 was active working either empty carriage stock in and out of Waterloo terminus or hauling passenger trains on the Clapham Junction-Kensington (Olympia) service. The end came for this engine in July, on the final day of Southern Region steam working. By the end of the month it had been cleared out of Nine Elms shed yard and taken to Salisbury for the scrap merchants to view and put in their bids. It was sold in October to a yard in South Wales alas not the one where dozens of resurrections took place. *David Dalton.*

Birkenhead shed became the home for many of the 9Fs during the latter days of steam traction on British Railways. Amongst the dozens which eventually ended up at 6C, eight of the converted Crosti engines managed to eke out a living at the former Joint GWR/LMS depot. This is No.92020 on the shed yard in 1966. This particular engine arrived here in January 1965 and was followed by Nos.92021 (July 65), 92022 (February 67), 92023 (July 65), 92024 (July 65), 92025 (February 67), 92026 (May 65), 92029 (December 66). This latter engine had been allocated to Birkenhead before, in November 1963, but had moved on to Saltley five months later. No.92028 had also been a resident of 6C at the same time as No.92029 and followed that engine to Birmingham where it was eventually withdrawn. Only No.92027 was never allocated to the Wirral depot but it wasn't many miles away being resident at a depot on the other side of the Mersey at Speke Junction. One of the longest and most arduous duties undertaken by the Birkenhead '9s' was the daily oil trains from Stanlow to Healey Mills and one to Leeds. Two engines were employed on the out (loaded to over one thousand tons) and empty return workings. Birkenhead crews would change over with Edgeley crews at Stockport, the timings were such that the westbound empty tank train with its twin ten-coupled motive power got to Edgeley to meet the eastbound train. Up to that point the engines had it pretty easy with just a very gradual rise from near sea level to Stockport but once the Manchester conurbation was left behind the work started in earnest to get the heavy load up to and then through the 3-mile long bore of Standedge tunnel. It could be said that those 9Fs working the oil trains went out in a blaze of glory - they certainly gave their all on that job. *David Dalton.*

No.70047, the only 'Britannia' never to carry a name. Surely anything would have done to complete the class - Pebble Mill at One! Steel Works of Lindsay! Perhaps the team which doled out the names for the 'Brits' were not as flippant or naive as those who took on the task during the diesel era. Anyway here it is at Chester, 2nd August 1955. Apparently quite a photographic rarity amongst the class, which just goes to show that everyone loves a namer - well most of them. *Ron Hodge.*

Lostock Hall shed became the final working depot for many steam locomotives during those final years leading up to August 1968. Indeed many through out their fires at that depot on that fateful August day when the End finally arrived. Cl.2 No.78020 was not amongst that number - Stanier's six and eight coupled locomotives ruled during those final days - and actually dropped its fire in May 1967 along with No.78021, the front end of which is just visible on the left of the picture. To say that No.78020 is in a sorry state would be an understatement but somebody has taken the trouble to clean the grime away from its cab side number for the benefit of visiting enthusiasts and photographers. Two other Cl.2s were 'on the books' at Lostock Hall - 78037 and 78041 - and these too were also withdrawn in May 1967. The exLMS Cl.3 0-6-0T with a lamp post appearing to sprout out of its chimneyless smokebox is No.47326. *David Dalton.*

Britannia No.70006 stables at the southern end of Crewe South shed at some time during 1967. By now nameless, the Pacific appears to have had a visit to Crewe works where a rough coat of green paint has been applied - no more niceties, no more lining. Even in this austere livery the 'Brits' still 'looked the business' especially from this rear three-quarter angle. One of the original Great Eastern line engines, No.70006 transferred to Carlisle Kingmoor in December 1963 after two months in store at March. Most of the former GE line Pacifics spent the latter part of 1963 stored at March shed before they too travelled to the greener pastures of Kingmoor. Their usual route during transfer to the north was via the East Coast main line to Gateshead then west over the Newcastle-Carlisle route. Spotters in the north-east had an early Christmas that year as most of the 'Brits' involved in this exodus had never visited the area before. *David Dalton.*

Even with its draughting problems DUKE OF GLOUCESTER was still able to perform on the WCML (what if it had done so to its real potential?) and one of its regular duties was taking the Down *MID-DAY SCOT* on to the north from its afternoon Crewe stop. It also worked the Up train to Euston and next day worked the Down train as far as Crewe. Here at Crewe North shed it is ready and prepared today for its northbound task whilst a group of enthusiasts gather to watch its departure to the station. Note the dilapidated roof of the shed which remained in that state until closure. *David Dalton.*

Its amazing how many BR Standard locomotives ended their days working on the Southern Region; a lot more than the number that started life on the Region. Class 4 No.76005 was one of those that actually started and finished its working life on the SR. This was the BR version (with many subtle differences of course) of the LMS 'Flying Pig' Ivatt Cl.4 2-6-0, which class incidentally was still being delivered from Doncaster when the Standard version was being erected at Horwich and Doncaster. Our subject here was one of the Horwich built engines delivered to Eastleigh in December 1952 before moving on to Bournemouth shed in July 1953. In May 1954, after five months at Brighton, No.76005 transferred to Dorchester and it was while the 2-6-0 was shedded there that photographer David Dalton captured it on film entering Bournemouth station with empty stock in August 1954. It was at Bournemouth where the Cl.3 did its final work before withdrawal in July 1967. The Wilberforce Hotel in the left background appears to be somewhat rundown, the lettering of the gable sign reminding this writer of the opening scene for each episode of Fawlty Towers! *David Dalton.*

9F No.92006 at Newport Ebbw Junction shed, 21st August 1955. When Crewe turned out the first examples of the 9F 2-10-0s in January 1954, they were destined for the Western Region. The WR allocation comprised the first eight engines (Nos.92000 to 92007) and they had all arrived on the Region by the end of February. Only one depot was to receive the newcomers - Ebbw Junction at Newport. Now, it is a fact of life that most human beings do not like change and the same can be said about animals too - routine, food, habitat, rules, virtually everything. Something new is change. A BR Standard 9F 2-10-0 is a change from a Collett 2-8-0 or indeed anything with a copper capped chimney and brass cabside numberplates! The new locomotives did not go down well at all. Add to the equation 'built at Crewe' and virtual racism surfaces amongst the crowd brought up on everything made in Swindon. Such was the reception given to the 9Fs that this batch for the WR were temporarily withdrawn whilst the gripes and moans of the footplate crews were received and then digested by the authorities. However, the WR authorities themselves were hardly enthusiastic about the 2-10-0s so the footplatemen had a most unlikely ally in their bosses. Long before the arrival of the 9Fs on WR metals the Paddington lot had tried in January 1953 to divert the forthcoming ten-coupled engines to other regions in favour of Swindon turning out - for the Western region of course - further Churchward designed 2-8-0 tender engines. So, the scene was set. Nobody on the former GWR wanted the new fangled BR Standards for goods service. There were two problems with the new engines one involving the brakes, the other was the regulator. Much has been written about those manifestations occurring but basically the steam brakes tended to take longer than necessary to react whilst the regulator stuck. Perhaps the Ebbw Junction men had a point after all. A few minor collisions resulted and the engines were stored pending rectification which duly took place. Our photograph was taken some eighteen months on and by this time the 9Fs had been accepted and were working the heavy iron ore trains from Newport docks to the Ebbw Vale steel works. Another eight new 9Fs arrived at Ebbw Junction shed in 1958, ironically they too were Crewe built, the Swindon products being destined for the Eastern Region. Most of the initial batch of engines worked from Ebbw Junction until the early 60's, No.92006 left in September 1963 for York but ended its working life at Wakefield in April 1967. *KRP 95F4.*

Back at Swindon works to see the release of another new 9F, we have No.92208 ready to earn a living on 6th June 1959. Its first shed was Laira in Plymouth and it was due to go there with sister No.92209 that same month. A few running-in turns from Swindon shed would no doubt position the engine to be pointing the right way because as it stands now the tender first running into deepest Devon would be somewhat taxing for its crew. Swindon still had another dozen 2-10-0s to complete not only their last new steam locomotive but also British Railways last. Crewe had put their final 9F into traffic during the previous December so ending their long association with steam locomotive building. On paper Swindon appeared reluctant to finish the job, dragging their heels somewhat. No.92210 came out in August after the works holiday, 11 and 12 during September, 13 and 14 in October, 15 in November, 16 and 17 during December, 18 and 19 were put out in January 1960 whilst No.92220 did not see the light until March albeit that it was being given special treatment and an official send-off. No.92208 got neither and ended its days at Carlisle Kingmoor where it arrived in June 1964. Withdrawal took place in November 1967. *David Dalton.*

To end our coverage of the 9Fs, lets take a look at one of them in passenger service. This is No.92184 of New England in the summer of 1958 setting out from York with a morning York-Bournemouth express. The booked motive power had obviously failed hence this little job for the 'space ship'. The train would travel via the GC main line but where the 9F came off the train is unknown. This wasn't the only passenger train this particular engine hauled that summer; in August it was seconded to work an Edinburgh-King's Cross express from Grantham. *KRP 241.8.*

Staying at York, we travel to the northern end of the shed yard to look at Cl.3 2-6-2T No.82027 sitting near the turntable. The date is May 1963 and the Cl.3, along with two of its sisters, has been just about everywhere on the North Eastern Region looking for work. Ex Swindon in November 1954, No.82027 had been longing for long term employment ever since. It was one of four allocated new to the NER (82026-82029) and spent its first four years at Kirkby Stephen along with No.82026. In January 1958 the pair moved temporarily to Darlington where they met up with 82028 and 82029. The event was brief because 82027, along with 82029 were sent to West Hartlepool. The others remained at Darlington until September 1958 when they transferred to Scarborough. At the same time our subject here along with 82029 went to Malton. Another brief encounter between the intrepid four took place at Scarborough from June 1960 until September 1961 when 82028 and 82029 were required at Malton. 82026 and 82027 remained at the seaside for another season but in December 1962 they both moved on, 82027 back to Malton and 82026 to Low Moor. By April 1963 the trio at Malton were no longer needed so they moved on to York. Not all of them were active for the five months they spent at 50A so this view of 82027 in steam was a bonus. At the end of the summer timetable all three of the York lot were sent away to the Southern where the old M7 tank engines were falling like flies and new blood was required. They landed at Guildford where once again they met up with 82026 which had come from Copley Hill and an unhappy time at Low Moor. After this the four amigos stayed together and in January 1964 Bournemouth had their company until the following September when they all went to Nine Elms to work the empty stock trains in and out of Waterloo. We will leave the happy little group at 70A where their eventual demise took place but not alas as a group. *KRP 245.5.*

Wearing a wrong facing BR emblem, No.82013 is seen passing one of the coal stacks at Exmouth Junction shed circa 1961. 72A had fourteen of this class delivered new, ten during the period from June to September 1952 (Nos.82010 to 82019), and Nos.82022 to 82025 during October and November 1954. Besides working the Southern branch lines in the vicinity of Exeter, the 2-6-2Ts also worked the lines in north Devon and Cornwall besides helping out with the banking duties from Exeter's St Davids station to Central station. It is no wonder then that the Exmouth Junction engines apparently recorded some very high mileages compared to the rest of the class. there was virtual full employment for them, at least whilst allocated to the Exeter depot. No.82013 transferred to Eastleigh in September 1962 but within a few months had gone to Nine Elms where most of the Southern Region members of the class ended their days. Withdrawal came fairly early for this engine and by the end of 1964 it was destined for a scrap yard in Kettering. *KRP 222.1.*

Having yet to acquire a Kirkby Stephen shed plate, Class 3 No.82026 is just about to depart Darlington (Bank Top) with the 10.15 a.m. morning service to Penrith in April 1955. Note the shields - quite prominent from this angle - protecting the two mechanical lubricators on the running plate. *Ron Hodge.*

Looking rather depleted and helpless, 7P No.70041 SIR JOHN MOORE waits to enter Stratford works on 25th May 1955, for remedial treatment to a big problem! Just what had gone wrong with the wheel or axle is unrecorded but the set of wheels within the adjacent wagon do not belong to the Britannia. No.70041 was a Stratford based member of the class and you can easily tell at a glance. *Ron Hodge.*

Another of the Stratford batch of 'Britannias' was No.70005 JOHN MILTON seen here departing Preston in April 1955 with what must be a northbound running-in turn after attention at Crewe. No stranger to the WCML, this Pacific spent some time at the Rugby Testing station in late 1952 and early 1953. For a 30A engine No.70005 looks fairly respectable but it had been through works for an Intermediate repair. *Ron Hodge.*

The time is 1.35 p.m. on 1st October 1955. The last few passengers from the Up working of *THE MANCUNIAN* are strolling down the platform after their arrival at Euston. Of all the Manchester (London Road) to London (Euston) expresses, this mid-morning 'flyer' was the lightest with never more than ten bogie coaches as opposed to *THE COMET* or *THE LANCASTRIAN* which normally had twelve bogies but were often strengthened to fourteen or more vehicles, as were the unnamed expresses plying between Euston and Manchester. Longsight 'Brit' No.70033 CHARLES DICKENS would have found this an easy chore with only one intermediate stop at Wilmslow. This particular locomotive was allocated to 9A for seven years before the coming of English Electric diesels and then electrification put paid to steam on these services. *Ron Hodge.*

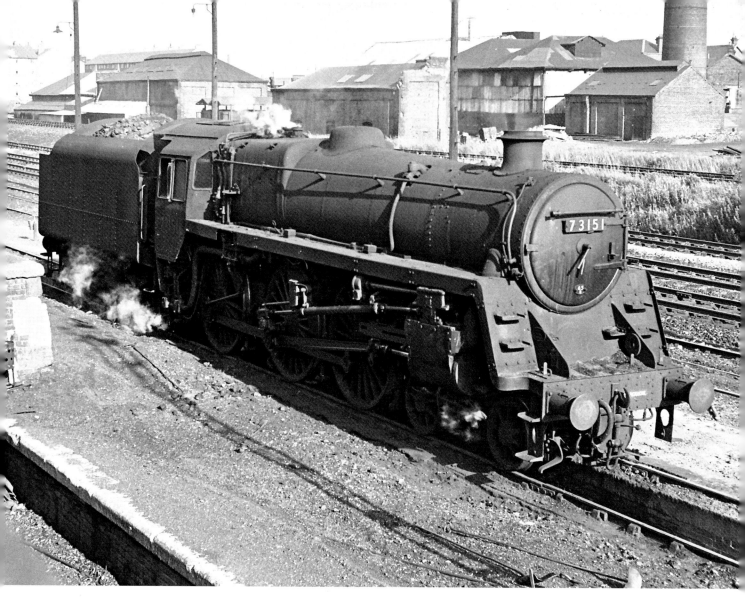

The midday sun highlights the coating of grime worn by one of the St Rollox Caprotti fitted Cl.5s, No.73151, in August 1965. The engine is standing on the ash pits area of the depot, alongside the main line to Glasgow's Buchanan Street station. The coaling stage - St Rollox was never blessed with mechanical coaling apparatus - stood just to the left of the picture and it would appear that No.73151 was just about to visit the stage to top its depleted tender. The '5' has obviously just reversed up from the terminus after working in from Dundee with a passenger train. After coaling it would continue reversing for another few hundred yards or so before proceeding forwards into the shed yard where a visit to the turntable would point the engine in the right direction for its next passenger working. just eight years old on the date of this photograph, No.73151 had exactly twelve months of working life before withdrawal and eventual scrap. One of ten Caprotti fitted Class 5s (73145 to 73154) delivered new to St Rollox in 1957, No.73151 spent the whole of its short life working from the Glasgow depot. *DHB 7661.*

Cl.5 No.73077 accelerates away from Fort William with a train for Glasgow (Queen Street) in July 1959. The engine has yet to acquire the large 10in. cabside numerals associated with Cowlairs and St Rollox workshops so presumably No.73077 has yet to attend either of those works for some major attention. Based at Eastfield shed, along with No.73078, since new in May 1955, the 4-6-0 also shared these West Highland line duties with Nos.73105 to 73109 after their arrival at Eastfield when new in late 1957 and early 1958. Although not recorded as such, this train was probably the 2.56 p.m. departure, the 4-6-0 having arrived from Glasgow on the 5.45 a.m. departure from Queen Street. Like their former LMS counterparts, the BR Cl.5s were well liked on this line, the reliability of the engine along with the cab comforts being appreciated by footplatemen. *KRP 234.6.*

In the days when they were turned out in a respectable external condition, two of Polmadie's five resident 'Brits', No.70051 FIRTH OF FORTH and 70052 FIRTH OF TAY, grace the shed yard at 66A in April 1957. Both engines are fuelled and turned ready to work southbound expresses. Of the five (70050 to 70054) which arrived new at Polmadie between August and October 1954, as the last engines of the third and final batch built, only No.70050 and these two stayed until April 1962, the others left in October 1958 for Leeds Holbeck and never returned. Though built at Crewe, the names for these last five were fitted at St Rollox works immediately after their journey from the south. Like all of the third batch engines (70045-70054), the Polmadie 'five' were coupled to the huge BR1D tenders which weighed-in at nearly 55 tons when full and were fitted with coal pushers. *DHB 3386.*

Just eighteen months old, Class 3 No.77006 at Hamilton shed in September 1955. During its somewhat short lifetime of twelve years, this engine resided at the following sheds: Hamilton - eight and a half years; Carstairs - one year; Grangemouth - nearly two years; Motherwell - five months, most of which were spent 'in store.' In this view it is difficult to define the lining afforded these engines when built, the tender especially has a nice coating of grime and it is obvious that this engine has not been treated to cleaning of any kind whilst at 66C. Of the above named depots, only Carstairs used its small contingent on anything worthy of a modern and reasonably powerful steam locomotive - fitted freights to Carlisle, along with local trips. Hamilton shed employed its pair - No.77007 was the other - on suburban passenger services into Glasgow and goods trip workings. Dieselisation was fast becoming a reality at Hamilton and No.77006 was ousted out in November 1962 which was quite late because its stablemate was got rid to Polmadie of in September 1959. Built at Swindon in March 1954, No.77006 was cut up at the Wishaw plant of Motherwell Machinery & Scrap in late 1966. *DHB 3647.*

Monday, 31st August 1959. York motive power depot. The evening sun highlights Cl.3 No.77012 which is buffered up to a WD 2-8-0 in the shed yard. This particular 2-6-0 spent the whole of its working existence on the North Eastern Region. Built at Swindon and released to traffic in June 1954, it was one of ten (half the class) allocated to various sheds within the NER. No.77012 first went to Darlington - they all did in fact - before being doled out to West Auckland in August. Just in time for the winter chill coming off the North Sea, the Class 3 transferred to Whitby during November 1958. That cab was so comfortable that the Whitby lads were loathe to let the engine go but they had to in December 1958 when York acquired it for the first time. In September 1963 No.77012 started what could be described as a four year long mini-tour of the NE Region and its depots - south, west, east , north and finally back to York in 1966 where it apparently became a favourite to haul the Inspection saloon! Condemned in June 1967, the thirteen year old 2-6-0 Cl.3 was taken southwards from whence it came but only got as far as Chesterfield where it was shunted into a scrap yard to face oblivion. *KRP 246.3.*

Working on the West Coast Main Line and approaching Penrith, 'Clan' No.72003 CLAN FRASER has charge of the 9.30 a.m. Manchester (Victoria) to Edinburgh express on 23rd June 1956. This Polmadie engine was one of the casualties of the class which went for an early withdrawal after months of storage and years of moaning and indecision. After the mass withdrawal of 29th December 1962, all of the Polmadie batch, Nos.72000 to 72004, went to Darlington for breaking up and at least one of them still had the BR lion and wheel emblem on the tender at the time of scrapping. Amazingly, and this gap between dates highlights everything that was wrong with BR at the time, the Kingmoor batch Nos.72005 to 72009 were not withdrawn for another two years and more! *Ron Hodge.*

With steam to spare, a pleasingly clean Polmadie 'Clan' No.72002 CLAN CAMPBELL, picks up water on 23rd June 1956 from Dillicar troughs in the Lune valley. The Pacific was working a Glasgow (Central) to Liverpool (Exchange) express. *Ron Hodge.*

Nine Elms shed 20th April 1967. One of the NE Region Class 3 'quads', No.82029, has arrived at its final home in south London. The only place to go from here is the scrap yard because nobody else wants the 2-6-2Ts. Withdrawal took place on 9th July when all the other steam in this part of London and throughout the Southern Region came to a grinding halt! *David Dalton.*